HEALED: ONCE AND FOR ALL

BY
ROD PARSLEY

HEALED: ONCE AND FOR ALL

BY
ROD PARSLEY

RESUL*T*S
PUBLISHING

Healed: Once and for All
By Rod Parsley
Published by Results Publishing
World Harvest Church, PO Box 100
Columbus, OH 43216-0100, USA
www.RodParsley.com

Unless otherwise noted, all scripture references are taken from the New King James Version of the Bible. Scripture quotations marked AMP are from THE AMPLIFIED BIBLE. The Amplified New Testament Copyright © 1958, 1987 by the Lockman Foundation. Used by permission.

ISBN: 1-933336-87-0
Printed in the United States of America

TABLE OF CONTENTS

HEALED: ONCE AND FOR ALL
INTRODUCTION

Hebrews 9:12 says, "Not with the blood of goats and calves, but with His own blood He entered the Most Holy Place once for all, having obtained eternal redemption." No serious Christian denies that redemption includes forgiveness of sin and an eternal home in heaven. But many believers hesitate when asked about the additional benefits of redemption, and some have difficulty accepting healing as a part of God's plan for them.

But there is no denying that God made our bodies as well as our spirits, and He wants our bodies to be well just as He wants our hearts to be cleansed from sin. The redemptive work of Jesus on the cross purchased our return to the original state — free from sin, sickness and every other factor that would keep us from accomplishing God's will.

Our covenant with God is guaranteed by nothing less than the life of Jesus Christ, the Lamb of God. The price He willingly paid purchased our freedom from death, disease and anything else that could limit or bind us. That sacrifice never has to be repeated — Jesus obtained our healing once and for all.

CHAPTER ONE
THREE QUESTIONS, ONE ANSWER

The Bible presents physical healing as a truth to be accepted and a fact to be understood rather an opinion to be debated or an option to be considered. Divine healing is a benefit provided by God for every believer, and those who refuse it fail to recognize it as the blessing God intended it to be.

Strangely enough, some in the body of Christ don't want to be associated with anything having to do with divine healing. These people are genuinely saved and on their way to heaven, but they tend to look at healing as a strange doctrine that is more superstitious and spooky than spiritual.

Even though divine healing has become a complex and complicated issue for many in the body of Christ, it is really very simple. In fact, there are only three main questions in the Bible that deal with divine healing.

The first question is: can God heal? This was the question asked by the man whose son who was held in the iron grip of bondage. He came to Jesus for help.

HEALED: ONCE AND FOR ALL

Mark 9:17-27 says:

Then one of the crowd answered and said, "Teacher, I brought you my son, who has a mute spirit. And wherever it seizes him, it throws him down; he foams at the mouth, gnashes his teeth, and becomes rigid. So I spoke to your disciples, that they should cast it out, but they could not."

He answered him and said, "O faithless generation, how long shall I be with you? How long shall I bear with you? Bring him to me."

Then they brought him to Him. And when He saw him, immediately the spirit convulsed him, and he fell on the ground and wallowed, foaming at the mouth. So He asked his father, "How long has this been happening to him?"

And he said, "From childhood. And often he has thrown him both into the fire and into the water to destroy him. But if you can do anything, have compassion on us and help us." Jesus said to him, "If you can believe, all things are possible to him who believes."

Immediately the father of the child cried out and said with tears, "Lord, I believe; help my un-

*belief!" When Jesus saw that the people came run-
ning together, He rebuked the unclean spirit, saying to it, "Deaf and dumb spirit, I command you,
come out of him and enter him no more!" Then
the spirit cried out, convulsed him greatly, and
came out of him.*

*And he became as one dead, so that many said,
"He is dead." But Jesus took him by the hand
and lifted him up, and he arose."*

The man said to Jesus, "If you can…," indicating his uncertainty regarding Jesus' ability to heal
his son. Jesus responded, "If you can believe…."
Another translation says, "It's not a matter of what
I can do; it's a matter of what you can believe."

And of course, we see the result — the boy
was made whole by the power of God. In this
case, the illness (which caused the boy to be mute
and have seizures) was the direct result of the
presence of a demonic spirit.

The reality of demon spirits and their activity
and influence is another subject that has been tho-
roughly treated elsewhere, but I need to mention
some things about the distinction between freedom from demonic influence and healing.

Please don't make the mistake of thinking that everyone who has seizures is demon-possessed, or that everyone who cannot speak is tormented by an evil spirit.

Many years ago a young man who attended our church had epilepsy, and would occasionally have a seizure at a church service or activity. Sometimes well-meaning but misinformed people would think that the seizure was a result of supernatural forces, when in fact it was nothing more than an involuntary interruption of some natural functions that caused him to convulse uncontrollably.

We eventually were able to educate most of our people about it, and when seizure activity occurred, they would stand by to make sure the young man didn't accidentally hurt himself or others, and stay with him until the episode passed. I am happy to report that the last time I heard from him, he had been seizure free for years.

Another man was unable to speak as a result of an unfortunate accident that had happened many years before. He would try to articulate words, especially when music was being sung or played, but was never able to utter more than a groan. His difficulty in vocalizing was only because the speech center of his brain had been damaged, not because of any kind of demonic activity.

Even though there are times when a person is sick because of the influence of a demon spirit, most of the time sickness is not the result of the direct operation of demon spirits. The Bible makes the distinction between casting out demons and healing.

Matthew 8:16 says:

When evening had come, they brought to Him many who were demon-possessed. And He cast out the spirits with a word, and healed all who were sick…

Another example is found in Matthew 10:1:

And when He had called His twelve disciples to him, He gave them power over unclean spirits, to cast them out, and to heal all kinds of sickness and all kinds of disease.

If demon spirits were directly responsible for all cases of sickness and disease, there would be no need to distinguish between healing and deliverance from demons. Let me say it again — sometimes sicknesses are the direct result of demonic activity, but most of the time they are not.

There is no question that God is able to heal
— He created the worlds, set the universe in mo-
tion, made the earth and everything that is in it. He
created your body out of dust, and He can fix
whatever is wrong with it. Our God is able.

God proved His ability to heal in Mark chapter
nine to the man and his son, as well as to all the
rest who were there on that occasion. Men can no
longer use the excuse that God is not able — He
proved that He is able, not only to heal, but to do
anything for which we can believe. If someone
doesn't get healed, it's not because God ran out of
healing power.

The next question people generally encounter
regarding divine healing is not whether or not God
is able to heal, but whether or not He is willing to
heal.

As with the question of His ability, we have an
example in the word of God from Mark 1:40-42,

> *Now a leper came to Him, imploring Him, kneel-*
> *ing down to Him and saying to Him, "If You are*
> *willing, You can make me clean." Then Jesus,*
> *moved with compassion, stretched out His hand*
> *and touched him, and said to him, "I am willing;*

be cleansed." As soon as He had spoken, imme-diately the leprosy left him, and he was cleansed.

I suppose that if someone was going to doubt anything about God, it would be better to doubt His ability than His willingness. Think about it — if someone needed your help, which question would deal with your credibility and character — doubt about your ability or doubt about your willingness to help them in a time of need?

This leper wasn't healed just because he was in a pitiful condition and Jesus felt sorry for him. There is a difference between feeling sorry for someone and having compassion on them. You can feel sorry for people all day long and never do anything to help them, but compassion compels you to action.

In the narrative we have of Jesus' life and ministry in the Gospels, in every case where an individual approached Him in need of healing, He always responded the same way: "I will." Not one time did He ever say, "No," or "Maybe," or "Wait," or "Let me think about it and get back to you."

How much clearer can God make His will concerning divine healing? Every time someone came to Jesus to be healed, God's answer in the pages of the Bible was a resounding, "Yes!"

Don't you think that if there were any exceptions to this, we would see them in the Bible? As many times as Jesus healed people, doesn't it stand to reason that if there was even one exception, we would see it in the word of God? Yet there isn't one.

A man decided he was going to settle the question of divine healing to his own satisfaction by taking a yellow marker and highlighting every passage in the Gospels where healing was included. Before long, he had a yellow Bible, and he realized that divine healing was God's will.

If God's people would be willing to do the same thing, and look at the Bible with eyes that weren't clouded by preconceived notions or religious thinking, they would come to the same conclusion.

The third and final question concerning divine healing is this: will you be healed? It is a question that men don't ask God, but that God asks men. Here is an example from John 5:2-3;5-6:

Now there is in Jerusalem by the sheep gate a pool, which is called in Hebrew, Bethesda, having five porches. In these lay a great multitude of sick people, blind, lame, paralyzed, waiting for the moving of the water... Now a certain man was there who had an infirmity thirty-eight years. When Jesus saw him lying there, and knew that he already had been in that condition a long time, He said to him, "Do you want to be made well?"

When Jesus saw him lying there, and knew that he already had been in that condition a long time, He said to him, "Do you want to be made well?"

Keep in mind that this man had been sick for 38 years. He was at the pool of Bethesda, which is where sick people were accustomed to going when they were seeking relief. Jesus came along and had the audacity to ask if he wanted to be well.

Just because someone is sick doesn't mean they want to be well. Sometimes they hold on to their infirmities because of the attention or emotional support they receive as a result of them.

I have met people who talk about their pains as though they were old friends or family members. You may know of someone who, when asked how they are doing, never fails to mention "old Arthur," meaning the arthritis that causes them pain every morning.

Others consider an infirmity not as an obstacle to be overcome, but as a means to financial gain. I vividly remember two examples of this that occurred years ago.

A staff member was answering the prayer phones and took a prayer request from a man who had a physical infirmity. The staff member told the man he would believe God with him for his healing. The caller told the staff member he didn't want to be healed, he just wanted a little relief from the pain. When the surprised staff member asked him why, the caller replied that if he got healed he would risk losing his government disability check.

I was walking through the halls of the church one afternoon when I sensed the healing anointing in an unusual way. I was near the office of a staff member who had told me he had chronic joint pain, so I stopped by and asked if I could lay hands on him and believe God for his healing. He declined, and explained that his bad knee was worth a lot of money to him due to an insurance settlement that hadn't yet been finalized.

Jesus didn't make any assumptions, but asked the man at the pool of Bethesda if he wanted to be healed. He asked the same thing of blind Bartimaeus outside of Jericho. The story is found in Mark 10:46-52. The man was blind, but when he appeared before Jesus, He asked him what he wanted.

It may have seemed obvious to those standing by what the blind man wanted, but Jesus waited to see what he said in response. It would have been a shame if Bartimaeus had said he wanted Jesus to heal a case of the sniffles, only to go on his way as blind as before!

Many people are asking God if He can heal and if He will heal, and all the while God is asking them if they want to be well. It would do us good to stop asking so many questions of God and answer the questions God is asking of us.

Before we move on, let's rehearse these three questions: Can God heal? Will God heal? Will you be healed? All three questions should have the same answer: Yes!

In addition to these three questions, there have always been three attitudes in the body of Christ concerning divine healing. The first and probably the most discredited is that God doesn't heal any longer.

The reason I say this attitude is discredited is because it is likely that someone you know has either experienced the healing power of God or knows someone who claims to have experienced it. God will even heal sinners, just because He loves them and wants them to know it.

I have prayed for many unbelievers who had some kind of physical symptoms that disappeared, sometimes even before the prayer was ended. In many cases, these people immediately gave their lives to the Lord because of the grace He demonstrated to them in His healing power.

To those who maintain that God doesn't heal any longer, I have this question: when did He stop? Was it when the last apostle died, or at some other time in history? If God ever healed anyone, He still heals today.

Some people don't want to talk about healing because they want to avoid any discussion or even thought about the supernatural, especially when it comes to their own lives. They are limited to what they can see with their eyes and hear with their ears.

Regardless of how much worldly wealth they acquire, they are among the poorest people on earth. They think that the only healing available to modern man is through medical science.

I certainly don't discredit the good that medical science can do and has done to help hurting people. I remember in excruciating detail the exquisite pain that coursed through every particle of my being when I experienced the movement of a tiny kidney stone inside my body.

I was dealing with a piece of calcium the size of a mustard seed, and I was looking for some relief, whether it came from mountain-moving faith or at the point of a pain-killing needle! We can all thank God for everything modern medicine is able to accomplish, but we should ultimately put our trust in God — and thank God, He is still healing today.

The next attitude in the church concerning divine healing is some variation of this religious sounding sentiment: God does heal, but only if it's His will. This sounds better than the first attitude, but it is basically an excuse used by those who don't know God's will but don't want people to think they don't believe God.

Some who have this attitude don't know any better and are just repeating something they have heard. In reality, this attitude has no basis in fact and only leads to doubt and unbelief.

The first question I always ask someone who has this attitude about healing is: "How do you know if it's His will?" The answer will nearly always be one of two things — either if you get healed, then it was God's will, or there's no way to know whether it's God's will.

Trial and error doesn't seem to me to be a very good way to determine God's will, especially when dealing with matters as important as our physical well-being. All we need to do to know God's will is read the Bible. We have already seen that every time someone came to Jesus for healing, His answer was always "Yes!"

This uncertainty about God's will leads people to believe that there has to be something special about them in order to get healed. They have to have a "lucky ticket" so to speak, in order to get anything from God. Of course, this idea has no scriptural basis.

God's truth is available to everyone, and His healing power will be manifested wherever His Word is believed. Healing is for everyone, not just a lucky few.

This leads us to the third attitude in the church concerning divine healing, and it is the scriptural one: God's will for healing is all-inclusive.

Make no mistake — God wants you to be well. This is the only conclusion that an unbiased examination of the word of God will yield.

God does not want you to be sick. God's will is for all His people to be well all the time, regardless of what kind of sickness or infirmity tries to attach itself to them.

The first objection people have to this point of view is, "If it's God's will for people to be well, why are so many people sick? If God wanted them to be well, they'd just be well!"

Again, that sounds religious on the surface, but consider it in light of forgiveness of sin. Does God want everyone to be saved? Of course He does. But is everyone saved? Obviously not. But if it's God's will for them to be saved, why wouldn't they just be saved? You can see the error in this objection to healing.

We understand that in order for someone to be saved, they must receive Jesus as their Savior. Regardless of how desperately God wants them to be saved, or how completely He has provided for their salvation, they have to do something to make salvation a reality in their own experience.

Everyone who trusts in Jesus as Savior will be saved. In order to appropriate the benefits God has provided for us, we must exercise faith in Him. This principle is the same regardless of what benefit we need from God. The reason people are not healed is not because God doesn't want them to be healed. The reason people are not healed is because they haven't met the conditions for healing.

Salvation never just hit anybody over the head as they were walking down the street. They had to receive Jesus as their Savior by faith. In the same way, healing won't just jump on anyone unannounced and uninvited. It must be received by faith.

One of the reasons some people have such trouble with this is because of an entitlement mentality — they think someone owes them everything. God owes us nothing — He is not indebted to us in any way. Anything we receive from Him is a matter of His grace extended toward us.

He loves us and wants us to be well in our physical bodies, which is why He offers us healing as a benefit of salvation. But if we have no faith, we will not be able to believe Him for healing or anything else that He has so graciously provided.

If we can find evidence of healing in the Bible as part of the redemptive purpose of God, then it won't be difficult for us to have faith in God for healing for our physical bodies. And that evidence is exactly what I want to show you next.

CHAPTER TWO
THE BURDEN BEARER

Unprecedented success often leads to unprecedented problems. At God's direction and with His divine aid, Moses was about to lead six million or more Israelites out of Egyptian captivity. But how would they be able to travel if many of them were weak from overwork or injured from mistreatment?

God already had a plan in mind, and we see it unfold in Exodus: 12:3-14:

Speak to all the congregation of Israel, saying: 'On the tenth of this month every man shall take for himself a lamb, according to the house of his father, a lamb for a household. And if the household is too small for the lamb, let him and his neighbor next to his house take it according to the number of the persons; according to each man's need you shall make your count for the lamb.

Your lamb shall be without blemish, a male of the first year. You may take it from the sheep or from the goats. Now you shall keep it until the fourteenth day of the same month. Then the whole assembly of the congregation of Israel shall kill it at twilight. And they shall take some of the blood and put it on the two doorposts and on the lintel of the houses where they eat it. Then they shall eat the flesh on that night; roasted in fire, with unleavened bread and with bitter herbs they shall eat it.

Do not eat it raw, nor boiled at all with water, but roasted in fire—its head with its legs and its entrails. You shall let none of it remain until morning, and what remains of it until morning you shall burn with fire. And thus you shall eat it: with a belt on your waist, your sandals on your feet, and your staff in your hand. So you shall eat it in haste. It is the Lord's Passover.

'For I will pass through the land of Egypt on that night, and will strike all the firstborn in the land of Egypt, both man and beast; and against all the gods of Egypt I will execute judgment: I am the Lord. Now the blood shall be a sign for you on the houses where you are. And when I see the blood, I will pass over you; and the plague shall not be on you to destroy you when I strike the land of Egypt.

'So this day shall be to you a memorial; and you shall keep it as a feast to the Lord throughout your generations. You shall keep it as a feast by an everlasting ordinance.

The Passover meal was not just an opportunity for them to eat before their trip began — it was the occasion for the healing power of God to flow through every Israelite who needed strength for the journey. Psalm 105:37 says:

> *He also brought them out with silver and gold, and there was none feeble among His tribes.*

The reason there was not one feeble among their tribes was because God healed them all before they left. Just as surely as the blood of the lamb protected them from the ravages of the destroying angel, the body of the lamb caused them to receive strength to walk out of Egypt and into their future. For six million people to be strengthened in one night is truly a miracle of Biblical proportions.

The Passover event is a type of the sacrifice of the Lord Jesus Christ, who gave His life so that we could be redeemed from the bondage of sin and the bondage of sickness. Paul identifies it this way in 1 Corinthians 5:7:

> *Therefore purge out the old leaven, that you may be a new lump, since you truly are unleavened. For indeed Christ, our Passover, was sacrificed for us.*

His sacrifice provided for our healing as well as for freedom from sin. This is just one of several notable examples in the Old Testament of how God foreshadowed His healing power that would be made available to all who believed in Jesus' sacrifice.

Every time a leper encountered Jesus and was healed in the Gospels, He would tell them to go show themselves to the priests. We see the reason for this in Leviticus 14:1-7:

> *Then the Lord spoke to Moses, saying, "This shall be the law of the leper for the day of his cleansing: He shall be brought to the priest. And the priest shall go out of the camp, and the priest shall examine him; and indeed, if the leprosy is healed in the leper, then the priest shall command to take for him who is to be cleansed two living and clean birds, cedar wood, scarlet, and hyssop. And the priest shall command that one of the birds be killed in an earthen vessel over running water. As for the living bird, he shall take it, the cedar wood and the scarlet and the hyssop, and dip them and the living bird in the blood of the bird that was killed over the running water. And he shall sprinkle it seven times on him who is to be cleansed from the leprosy, and shall pronounce him clean, and shall let the living bird loose in the open field.*

Two birds were taken, and one was killed, symbolizing death, but the other was released, symbolizing resurrection. Lepers were quarantined outside any place where people ordinarily lived or traveled.

They were relegated to a kind of living death. Their healing was little less than a resurrection — life again from the grave of separation and isolation. If healing was available for lepers under the old covenant, how much more should healing be available for those under the sentence of death today?

Here is another fascinating type of healing found in Leviticus 25:9:

Then you shall cause the trumpet of the Jubilee to sound on the tenth day of the seventh month; on the Day of Atonement you shall make the trumpet to sound throughout all your land.

Jubilee, of course, was the Jewish celebration of the fiftieth year, when debts were forgiven and everyone went back to their rightful possessions. Jesus announced the year of Jubilee in Luke 4:18-19:

The Spirit of the Lord is upon Me, because He has anointed Me to preach the gospel to the poor; He has sent Me to heal the brokenhearted, to proclaim liberty to the captives and recovery of sight to the blind, to set at liberty those who are oppressed; to proclaim the acceptable year of the Lord.

When Jesus made this declaration, no doubt the religious leaders looked at their calendars and said that the year of release was nowhere near. But Jesus was talking about a redemption that didn't come as a result of consulting a calendar, but as a result of believing in Him.

He came, to quote the prophet Isaiah, "to proclaim healing to the brokenhearted and recovering of sight to the blind." He set about to do just that during His earthly ministry, and is still doing that today. In fact, whatever had been lost was supposed to be regained during the year of Jubilee.

We lost our health due to sin, but whatever was lost in Adam is regained in Jesus Christ. Healing is one of our rightful possessions, and Jesus came to give it back to us. Here's another example from Numbers 21:5-9:

And the people spoke against God and against Moses: "Why have you brought us up out of Egypt to die in the wilderness? For there is no food and no water, and our soul loathes this worthless bread."

So the Lord sent fiery serpents among the people, and they bit the people; and many of the people of Israel died. Therefore the people came to Moses, and said, "We have sinned, for we have spoken against the Lord and against you; pray to the Lord that He take away the serpents from us."

So Moses prayed for the people. Then the Lord said to Moses, "Make a fiery serpent, and set it on a pole; and it shall be that everyone who is bitten, when he looks at it, shall live."

So Moses made a bronze serpent, and put it on a pole; and so it was, if a serpent had bitten anyone, when he looked at the bronze serpent, he lived.

We see from Jesus' own words that the bronze serpent was a type of His sacrifice, from John 3:14-15:

And as Moses lifted up the serpent in the wilderness, even so must the Son of Man be lifted up, that whoever believes in Him should not perish but have eternal life.

Jesus alludes to this again in John 12:32-33:

"And I, if I am lifted up from the earth, will draw all peoples to Myself." This He said, signifying by what death He would die.

Anyone in the camp of Israel who looked at the bronze serpent in faith and obedience received deliverance from the effects of the snakes that plagued the camp. In our day, anyone who looks upon the sacrifice of Jesus in faith and obedience will be delivered from the effects of the diseases that threaten them. In fact, the serpent upon a pole became so widely associated with healing that it is still a symbol used by the medical community to identify their mission.

We have been redeemed from the curse of the broken law, which involves three things — death as a result of sin, sickness of all kinds and poverty. Galatians 3:13-14 makes it clear:

Christ has redeemed us from the curse of the law, having become a curse for us (for it is written, "Cursed is everyone who hangs on a tree"), that the blessing of Abraham might come upon the Gentiles in Christ Jesus, that we might receive the promise of the Spirit through faith.

To *redeem*, as it is used in this passage, means *to buy out from under or away from*. It literally means *to return to the original state*. Our original state as God created us was free from sickness and disease.

It is beyond imagination to believe that there was any sickness in the Garden of Eden. Our redemption includes everything that was lost in the fall, including our physical health.

We see our redemption from death in passages such as Romans 5:21 and John 5:24. We see our redemption from poverty in places such as 2 Corinthians 8:9 and Luke 6:38.

God did not do a two-thirds job when it comes to our redemption. We are redeemed from sickness just as much as we are redeemed from sin or from poverty.

Here is an example from Luke 5:17-26:

Now it happened on a certain day, as He was teaching, that there were Pharisees and teachers of the law sitting by, who had come out of every town of Galilee, Judea, and Jerusalem. And the power of the Lord was present to heal them.

HEALED: ONCE AND FOR ALL

Then behold, men brought on a bed a man who was paralyzed, whom they sought to bring in and lay before Him. And when they could not find how they might bring him in, because of the crowd, they went up on the housetop and let him down with his bed through the tiling into the midst before Jesus.

When He saw their faith, He said to him, "Man, your sins are forgiven you." And the scribes and the Pharisees began to reason, saying, "Who is this who speaks blasphemies? Who can forgive sins but God alone?"

But when Jesus perceived their thoughts, He answered and said to them, "Why are you reasoning in your hearts? Which is easier, to say, 'Your sins are forgiven you,' or to say, 'Rise up and walk'?

"But that you may know that the Son of Man has power on earth to forgive sins" — He said to the man who was paralyzed, "I say to you, arise, take up your bed, and go to your house."

Immediately he rose up before them, took up what he had been lying on, and departed to his own house, glorifying God. And they were all amazed,

30

and they glorified God and were filled with fear, saying, "We have seen strange things today!"

Jesus told the man on the pallet that his sins were forgiven. After that, He told him to get up and go home. Neither was more difficult than the other, since the same redemptive work provided for both forgiveness of sins and healing of diseases. The man went home forgiven and healed.

Here is another example from Paul's teaching in 1 Corinthians 11:23-30:

For I received from the Lord that which I also delivered to you: that the Lord Jesus on the same night in which He was betrayed took bread; and when He had given thanks, He broke it and said, "Take, eat; this is My body which is broken for you; do this in remembrance of Me."

In the same manner He also took the cup after supper, saying, "This cup is the new covenant in My blood. This do, as often as you drink it, in remembrance of Me."

For as often as you eat this bread and drink this cup, you proclaim the Lord's death till He comes. Therefore whoever eats this bread or drinks this cup of the Lord in an unworthy manner will be guilty of the body and blood of the Lord.

But let a man examine himself, and so let him eat of the bread and drink of the cup. For he who eats and drinks in an unworthy manner eats and drinks judgment to himself, not discerning the Lord's body. For this reason many are weak and sick among you, and many sleep.

Paul lamented that many believers were weak and sick, and many had died prematurely as a result of not discerning the Lord's body. There is much I could say here about not properly discerning the Lord's body, but the thing I want to emphasize is that millions of believers have taken communion all their lives without understanding the benefit of healing that is available to them as a result of the sacrifice of the Lord's body.

We have already seen the example of Passover, and how the blood of the lamb and the flesh of the lamb provided the children of Israel with protection from death and healing from disease. In the same way, the fulfillment of that type in Jesus Christ provides us with protection from death

through His shed blood and healing for our bodies
through His broken body.

Matthew 8:16-17 says:

When evening had come, they brought to Him
many who were demon-possessed. And He cast
out the spirits with a word, and healed all who
were sick, that it might be fulfilled which was spo-
ken by Isaiah the prophet, saying: "He Himself
took our infirmities and bore our sicknesses."

Some try to relegate this example to Jesus pro-
viding healing for our spiritual sicknesses, but the
context here is Jesus dealing with physical sickness
and disease. In addition, Matthew refers to a well-
known passage of Scripture that points out the
substitutionary aspect of Jesus' work in carrying
our sicknesses as well as our sins. This is so important that we need to look at it in detail.

Isaiah 53:4-5 says this:

Surely He has borne our griefs and carried our sor-
rows; yet we esteemed Him stricken, smitten by
God, and afflicted. But He was wounded for our
transgressions, He was bruised for our iniquities;
the chastisement for our peace was upon Him, and
by His stripes we are healed.

I want to point out a few words in these verses that are vital to our understanding of the redemptive work of Jesus Christ. We understand, of course, that the subject of the entire chapter of Isaiah 53 is the Messiah, the Servant of Yahweh. He is seen as a burden bearer, similar to the scapegoat who symbolically bore the sins of Israel away to a desert place on the Day of Atonement.

In verse four, the prophet Isaiah uses the words *griefs* and *sorrows*. In the Hebrew language, the original language of most of the Old Testament, *griefs* is the word *choliy*, meaning *malady*, and is often translated *disease* or *sickness*. *Sorrows* is the word *makob*, meaning *anguish*, and is often translated *pain*.

If we use these definitions of these two words, the redemptive work of Jesus regarding healing becomes much clearer: "Surely He has borne our *diseases* and carried our *pain*...."

But there is even more these verses have to reveal about the complete redemption provided for us by Jesus on the cross. Notice the verbs that precede the words for sickness and pain in verse 4. "...He has *borne* our sicknesses and *carried* our pain...."

The word *borne* here is the Hebrew word *nasa*, which means to *lift*. It is used in the sense of bearing or carrying away, as a burden. The word *carried* is the Hebrew word *sabal*, which means to *carry*. It is used in the sense of bearing as a burden as well.

I'm not trying to turn you into a language student, but I don't want you to miss the significance of these words in connection with our redemption from sickness and disease.

These are the very same verbs that are used later in Isaiah chapter 53, specifically in verses 11 and 12, to describe the way the Messiah bore and carried our sins and iniquities.

In verse 12, the Bible says "...He bore (*nasa*) the sin of many...." In verse 11, it says "...He shall bear (*sabal*) their iniquities."

The very same words that are used to describe how Jesus Christ, the Messiah, carried our sins and iniquities are also used to describe how He carried our sicknesses and pains. It is clear that His substitutionary sacrifice provided for our redemption from both sin and sickness.

Verse five of this passage also yields some va-lu-able treasures regarding our redemption from sickness. Isaiah 53:5 quoted in 1 Peter 2:24, with a notable change of tense:

> *Who Himself bore our sins in His own body on the tree, that we, having died to sins, might live for righteousness — by whose stripes you were healed.*

As you can see, Isaiah says "we *are* healed" and Peter says "you *were* healed." The prophet, of course, was looking forward to Jesus' redemptive work, while Peter had the advantage of looking back on an already completed work, enabling him to identify something that had already taken place.

Peter also links the forgiveness of sins and the healing of diseases in the same context, which is consistent with what we have already seen elsewhere in the Word of God.

The Greek word Peter uses that is translated *healed* is *iamoai*, which means to *cure*, and is used 28 times in the New Testament, always referring to physical healing.

The word *stripes* in Isaiah 53:5 and 1 Peter 2:24 is also fascinating. The Greek word *molops* means a *blow-mark* or *bruise*. The word is singular, not plural, indicating that Jesus was not bruised separately, but that He was literally one big bruise as a result of the beating He received.

I believe we would have more appreciation for what Jesus provided for us if we had a better understanding of what it cost Him to purchase it. Let me summarize some of what Jesus endured to provide you with freedom from sickness and pain.

Following His arrest in the garden of Gethsemane, He was taken to the high priest's house and interrogated. Those present treated Him with unusual cruelty, including spitting on Him, striking Him and even hitting Him while He was blindfolded, mocking Him and asking Him to identify who hit Him. This was in fulfillment of Isaiah 50:6:

> *I gave My back to those who struck Me, and My cheeks to those who plucked out the beard; I did not hide My face from shame and spitting.*

After a long, lonely and sleepless night, Jesus was tried and found guilty of blasphemy and taken to the Roman governor, Pontius Pilate. Pilate sent Him to Herod, who sent Him back to Pilate, who turned Him over to the Roman soldiers to be scourged.

This scourging deserves further consideration, since there has been so much misinformation spread about it. You may have heard that Jesus received 39 stripes, or lashes as punishment before He was crucified. While it is true that Jewish law forbade beating anyone with more than 40 lashes, and according to tradition they subtracted one to guard against miscounting and breaking the law, we need to remember that Jesus was not scourged by Jews.

The Bible states that the scourging was carried out at the direction of Pilate by Roman soldiers. The marks Jesus received were not some little red welts across his back, as depicted in some cinematic portrayals of His suffering.

The best approximation I have seen is the scourging that Jesus received in the movie *The Passion of the Christ.*

What is not as well known is what happened to Jesus after He was beaten. In His bloody and weakened state, He was used as the object of a cruel game known as the game of the king. In it, the soldiers chose a prisoner from those who were sentenced to death and subjected him to the most degrading and inhumane insults imaginable before taking him away to the place of crucifixion.

I have stood upon the paving stones that made up the courtyard of the Pilate's judgment hall, now far below the street level of modern Jerusalem, where a crude game board was scratched into the floor. One line extended beyond the others in the diagram, which stopped at what looked like the figure of a sword.

I asked our tour guide about it, and she said that the longer line represented the victim's life, which was about to be cut short. I could almost hear the taunts and jeers of the soldiers as they mocked Jesus' divinity by putting a crown of thorns on His head, placing a reed in His hand to resemble a scepter, and throwing a robe over His shoulders.

Then they struck Him, spit on Him, and bowed before Him as though worshipping a king. He refused to dignify their insults with any response.

After some time, the soldiers put His own clothes back on Him and led Him away to be crucified. At first, they made Him carry the beam that would be the crosspiece of His cross, and later, when He faltered, forced a pilgrim along the street to carry it the rest of the way to Golgotha.

The crucifixion itself involved the victim being literally nailed to the cross, one spike through each wrist and one through the feet. Sometimes one spike was driven through each ankle on either side of the upright post. In either case, the victim literally hung there, and was forced to push himself up on his pierced feet to breathe.

Sometimes they lingered for hours and even days, but on this occasion the soldiers had orders to hasten death by breaking the victim's legs. Of course, Jesus, having been so terribly beaten, was already dead by that time, making such mutilation unnecessary. In a final indignity, one soldier pierced His side with a spear after His death.

Psalm 22:1-21 gives us a picture of what kind of suffering Jesus endured to purchase your healing and mine. I encourage you to read it carefully and thoughtfully to get a better idea of the price He paid to purchase your freedom from sickness as well as sin.

Isaiah 52:14 (AMP) gives us another dimension of what He went through to set you free from disease:

> *For many the servant of God became an object of horror; many were astonished at Him. His face and His whole appearance were marred more than*

any man's, and His form beyond that of the sons of men....

It cost God the life of His Son to set us free from the bondage of sickness. Healing is without a doubt a part of our redemption that was purchased once for all.

CHAPTER THREE
WAYS AND MEANS

God is a God of infinite variety. Even though His principles remain constant, He can and does use different means to accomplish His purposes. There are many ways God has used to provide healing for His people. I want to tell you about some of the most common ones.

One way God heals is through the laying on of hands. This is listed in Hebrews 6:2 as a fundamental principle of the doctrine of Christ, and is seen in the Bible in a number of different applications besides healing.

Laying on of hands has been used from ancient times to set people apart for a particular purpose or to transfer authority. God instructed Moses to have the children of Israel lay their hands on the Levites in Numbers 8:10. Moses himself laid his hands on Joshua in Numbers 27:18.

In the New Testament, the apostles laid hands on the deacons chosen to serve in the church at Jerusalem in Acts 6:6. The leaders of the church at Antioch laid hands on Paul and Barnabas before sending them on their first missionary journey in Acts 13:3.

Laying on of hands was also a way to minister the baptism of the Holy Spirit, as we see with the believers in Samaria in Acts 8:17. Ananias had a vision from the Lord directing him to find Saul of Tarsus and lay hands on him so that he might receive his sight and be baptized in the Holy Ghost (Acts 9:17). Paul laid his hands on believers at Ephesus, and they received the gift of the Holy Ghost as well in Acts 19:6.

Laying on of hands was also used to impart an anointing or to confirm a blessing, as seen in Jesus' ministry to the little children in Mark 10:16, as well as in 1 Timothy 4:14 and 5:22.

But the most common use of the ministry of laying on of hands was for healing. It was commonplace in Jesus' ministry. Over and over again the Gospels record Jesus laying His hands on the sick, as in Matthew 8:3 and 8:15, as well as Mark 6:5, 7:32, 8:23, and Luke 4:40. No doubt there were many other occasions when Jesus laid His hands on the sick that are not specifically recorded.

All believers are commissioned to lay hands on the sick by the head of the church, the Lord Jesus Christ in Mark 16:18. Jesus said healing was one of the signs that would follow believers as they laid hands on the sick. This doesn't require a degree in theology or any religious ritual or formal training — simple obedience is all that is necessary.

Jesus said in John 14:12: "Most assuredly, I say to you, he who believes in Me, the works that I do he will do also; and greater works than these he will do, because I go to My Father." One of the works Jesus did was to heal the sick. We can do the same thing if we will obey His instructions to lay hands on the sick.

Many times all a sick person needs is what has come to be known as a point of contact to release their faith. It can be very helpful to them to be able to point to a certain time when the healing power of God began to work in them, causing them to be well and whole.

There has been quite a lot of debate about how this actually works, but it's really not that complicated. Anyone who has ever touched a wire or other object with electrical current running through it can understand it.

When you make contact with the electrical current, what is in the wire gets in you, and it has an unmistakable effect on your body. If the current is strong enough or the contact is long enough, it can have an irreversible effect.

First John 2:20 says, "But you have an anointing from the Holy One...." This anointing that is in you comes from God and is the same anointing that was in Jesus. It can be transferred by contact with others, but with a very important provision — faith has to be involved. We know this from Jesus' encounter with the woman with the issue of blood in Mark 5.

The woman touched the hem of His garment, and He recognized that power had gone out of Him, but He did not know who touched Him until the woman came and fell at His feet and told Him what happened. No doubt there were a lot of people touching Him as He and His disciples pressed through the crowded streets, but there was one touch that was different, because it was a touch of faith, not of mere curiosity.

Sometimes the power of God can be felt. It's not always easy to explain spiritual things in natural terms, and those who have never had this experience may find it hard to understand, but there are times when God is healing people that you can literally sense the power of God going out of you and into those you touch. It's not necessary to feel anything to know something is happening, because we walk by faith and not by sight, but there are times when God uses a tangible touch to encourage those who need healing.

Whether you ever feel anything or not, it is important to obey Jesus' command to lay hands on the sick. You are not responsible to make them well — only God can do that — you are only responsible to obey the Word of the Lord.

I need to add a word of caution here. Be careful to use good sense and not get carried away by emotion and start doing inappropriate things when laying hands on the sick. All you have to do is touch them gently — don't be rough or harsh with people. You don't have to lay your hands on the afflicted part of their body — all you have to do is touch them. Many times all that is necessary is to take their hand—God will do the rest.

Another way God has provided for healing is through anointing with oil. In both the Old and New Testaments, olive oil was used as a balm or ointment, and in both Hebrew and Greek the word *anoint* means to *rub* or to *smear*.

In Genesis 28:18, Jacob anointed a pillar that he set up at Bethel as a memorial to God, since God gave him a vision in that place as he slept. God gave Moses the recipe for holy anointing oil which was to be used for the priests and the articles of worship in the tabernacle.

Lepers who were cleansed under the law were anointed with oil. Kings were anointed with oil, such as Saul in 1 Samuel 10:1. Later, David was anointed to be king in 1 Samuel 16:13.

In the New Testament, it was customary for hosts to anoint guests with oil as a courtesy, according to Luke 7:46. The Samaritan used oil in ministering to the wounded man in Luke 10:34.

Olive oil was common in Bible times, and was used as fuel for the lampstand in the tabernacle. It is still a staple in Middle Eastern households. People use it in cooking, on their hair and skin, to make soap, and for a number of other things. I have heard reports that some people even drink it.

Jesus commissioned His twelve disciples to go and preach in Mark chapter six. Verse 13 says:

...and [they] anointed with oil many who were sick, and healed them.

James 5:14-15 says:

Is anyone among you sick? Let him call for the elders of the church, and let them pray over him, anointing him with oil in the name of the Lord. And the prayer of faith will save the sick, and the Lord will raise him up...

Oil has traditionally been seen as an abiding reminder of the presence and activity of the Holy Spirit. The oil that has historically been used in ministering to the sick has been olive oil, but if no olive oil is available, any kind of oil will do. There is nothing about the oil in itself that causes people to be healed. As the above passage in James indicates, faith is what is necessary, regardless of the means of healing used.

I have used corn oil or some other kind of cooking oil on a number of occasions, and have heard of people using motor oil when nothing else was at hand.

It isn't necessary to use a lot of oil — just enough to make sure the person receiving ministry knows they have been touched. It is usually convenient to apply the oil to the forehead, although where the oil is placed is not as important as the faith that is released when it is applied. Don't despair if no oil is available; there are other ways God has provided for people to be healed.

Another familiar means of healing is the prayer of agreement. Matthew 18:19-20 says:

Again I say to you that if two of you agree on earth concerning anything that they ask, it will be done for them by My Father in heaven. For where two or three are gathered together in My name, I am there in the midst of them.

The word *agree* here is the Greek word *sumphoneo*, which means to be *harmonious* — which is where we get our word *symphony*. It means that we are all playing the same tune — that we are in agreement.

We see the principle of agreement from Deuteronomy 32:30, which says:

How could one chase a thousand, and two put ten thousand to flight, unless their Rock had sold them, and the Lord had surrendered them?

The context here indicates that Israel's enemies could not overcome them unless they had done something to get out from under the Lord's protection, but what I want to point out is the multiplication principle involved. Two cannot do just twice as much as one; two can do ten times as much as one — if they are in agreement.

Jesus promised us that if we would agree, He would be there in our midst to do whatever we asked. He didn't say He would get there when we prayed, He said He would already be there when we prayed. That's a good foundation for faith.

And truly being in agreement is the key to the success of this method of healing. The two who are praying really need to be in agreement, and not just give the appearance of being in agreement.

It is best if the prayer of agreement for healing can be prayed with the person who desires healing. If that is not possible, such as in the case of someone who is hospitalized or who lives some distance away, the next best option is to agree with someone who is close to the one needing healing.

In either case, it is always a good idea to find out what they believe before you pray. In most instances it won't take long before they will say something that will let you know whether or not they are acting in faith, or whether they are just trying something to see if it might work.

There have been many occasions when I have prayed with people, and after prayer, they would look at me and say something like, "Well, I sure hope this works." I can tell them right then that it didn't, because they were only hoping and I was believing. We were not in agreement.

Here's a word of caution for those who use the prayer of agreement: beware that you don't spend all your time praying for those who never pray for themselves. Some people have the idea that anyone in any kind of leadership in the body of Christ has great faith and God always hears them.

On the other hand, the same people tend to believe their own prayers are seldom heard and answered. As a result, they ask others to pray about things they never pray about themselves.

The effect of this is they never feel compelled to develop their own faith in God, and if something doesn't happen the way they think it should, they can always blame someone else without feeling any personal responsibility themselves.

I believe the prayer of agreement is best used when someone has had difficulty getting an answer to prayer themselves due to an unusual or extra-ordinary circumstance, or when a crisis threatens them and they need additional support. Many situations will respond to an individual's faith if they will just exercise it. The prayer of agreement can be used for situations where they need additional spiritual leverage to get it to move.

An additional caution is relevant here as well: choose your prayer partners carefully. Not everyone feels the need to be discreet with the information you share with them about your prayer needs. More than a few relationships have been strained because of public revelations about personal matters intended to be kept private in prayer.

If someone you know has a need to tell what they know, or even worse, what they think they know, choose someone else as your prayer partner, regardless of how powerful they appear to be in prayer.

One more word about the prayer of agreement: you have to articulate what you want in order for someone to agree with you. Years ago in prayer meetings, some people would ask for prayer for what they called "unspoken requests." This sounds religious, but is really not scriptural. How can we agree if I don't know what we are agreeing about?

When Jesus stopped on the road outside Jericho and asked blind Bartimaeus what he wanted, the beggar didn't say, "I have an unspoken request." Nobody ever got anything at the fast food drive through by pulling up to the menu board and announcing, "Unspoken request!"

I realize there are times when your heart may be overwhelmed with grief or some other conflict, but it is likely that you need some other kind of prayer during those times. In order to have the prayer of agreement, you have to say what you want.

Another means God has provided for healing is the manifestation gift of the Spirit known as the gifts of healings. There are nine of these gifts in all, listed in 1 Corinthians 12:8-10:

> *...for to one is given the word of wisdom through the Spirit, to another the word of knowledge through the same Spirit, to another faith by the same Spirit, to another gifts of healings by the same Spirit, to another the working of miracles, to another prophecy, to another discerning of spirits, to*

*another different kinds of tongues, to another the
interpretation of tongues.*

A thorough study of these gifts is an entire
book in itself, but let me summarize a few points.
As you can see from the above list, there are nine
of these gifts. I call them manifestation gifts to distinguish them from the ministry gifts listed in
Ephesians 4:11 and the motive gifts listed in Romans 12:6-8.

Dr. Howard Carter, a British scholar and missionary, studied these gifts extensively and suggested that they be understood and arranged in
three categories.

There are three power gifts, which are faith,
gifts of healings and working of miracles. There
are three revelation gifts, which are the word of
wisdom, the word of knowledge and discerning of
spirits. There are three vocal gifts, which are
prophecy, different kinds of tongues and the interpretation of tongues.

The gifts of healings can be defined as supernatural healing of sickness or disease without natural aid of any kind. This gift is distinguished from
the working of miracles, which is supernatural in-

tervention into or suspension of the laws of nature.

Miracles tend to be more creative in nature, where healings involve the restoration of a damaged or diseased organ or body part, sometimes over a period of time, and at times contingent on continued obedience to God.

I certainly don't mean to draw artificial and unnecessary distinctions between miracles and healings — the only reason I am pointing out the difference is to help define the gift. Some things in the Bible are identified as miracles of healing, such as the man who was healed at the Beautiful gate of the Temple in Acts 4:22. I'm sure the man didn't care whether it was a miracle or a healing; he was just glad to be able to walk again.

The gifts of healings are always mentioned in the Bible in plural form. Why this is so is not specifically stated, and has led to much speculation on the part of Bible scholars. Some have suggested that there is a gift of healing for every type of sickness or disease. We may never know with certainty whether or not this is the case.

What I have observed is that different people seem to have different degrees of success ministering to those who are afflicted with certain ailments.

One may see more results in ministering to those who have heart conditions. Another may have better results ministering to people afflicted with cancer. Some seem to have a particularly strong anointing to minister to the deaf or hearing impaired. Others have a remarkable ability to minister healing to those who have had difficulty conceiving.

First Corinthians 12:11 gives us a key to the operation of all the gifts of the Spirit:

> *But one and the same Spirit works all these things, distributing to each one individually as He wills.*

Nobody can make the gifts of the Spirit operate; they occur as the Holy Spirit wills. There are some things people can do to prevent the gifts of the Spirit from operating — disobedience being the main one.

If we never obey Jesus' command to lay hands on the sick, we will very likely never see the gifts of healings in operation. But the more we obey God in this area, the more likely we are to see this gift in operation.

This gift was very likely at work in the case of the paralyzed man at the pool of Bethesda. There was a multitude of sick people there, but on this occasion, we only have record of Jesus ministering to one. Why? We simply don't know, and any efforts to explain it would just be guesswork.

What we must avoid doing is getting sidetracked with wondering about what hasn't happened, and focus instead on what can happen. Regardless of whether or not a particular gift of the Spirit is in operation, we are not without options.

In fact, when Jesus Himself was limited by the unbelief of those in His hometown, He did what He could. Mark 6:5-6 says:

Now He could do no mighty work there, except that He laid His hands on a few sick people and healed them. And He marveled because of their unbelief. Then He went about the villages in a circuit, teaching.

Regardless of what gifts are operating or what miracles may or may not be taking place, two things you can always do to minister to the sick are lay hands on them, as Jesus did here, and teach them. Teaching may not be as emotional or as demonstrative as preaching, but it destroys unbelief.

Sometimes we look for the spectacular, such as signs, wonders and notable miracles. But if we wait for those things, we may well miss the other ways that God moves among His people. Let's remain open to be used by God however He sees fit to use us, and let's always be ready to move in any way God directs us to move.

CHAPTER FOUR
MORE WAYS AND MEANS

In the previous chapter, we took a look at four ways God uses to provide healing. God is certainly not limited to four — there are others. I want to point out three more ways that healing is available.

As we discussed earlier, the Jewish feast of Passover commemorated the miraculous deliverance of Israel from the bondage of slavery in Egypt.

Passover was a type of the substitutionary sacrifice of the Lamb of God, the Lord Jesus Christ. When Jesus partook of the Passover with His disciples, He told them that the bread they partook of was His body, and the cup they drank was the cup of the New Testament in His blood.

This demonstrates that Jesus was the fulfillment of the truth of which Passover was only a type — God had provided forgiveness from sin and healing from sickness for His people.

Communion is another vehicle God has provided for healing. In fact, Paul warned believers that if they did not recognize the Lord's body, they would risk being sick and dying prematurely.

Communion is generally regarded as a funeral meal, when it should be seen as cause for celebration. If Jesus were still dead, we might mourn His passing, but He is alive, and because He is alive, we have life. But the life He died and rose again to give us is not a sick, weak, broken-down existence. He came to give us life, and life more abundantly. We ought to act like it!

Every time you partake of communion, remember the price Jesus paid to purchase not only your salvation from sin, but your salvation from sickness. I realize we don't usually think of it in those terms, but salvation is exactly what we need from sickness.

We need to be saved from the diseases that threaten to weaken and eventually kill our mortal body. That is exactly what God has provided through communion. Take it often. Take it sincerely. But take it joyfully, knowing that a loving God has provided a means of healing that will work for you just as much as it worked for the Israelites coming out of Egypt so many years ago.

Another means of healing God has given us is what I call special anointings. Before I go into more detail about this, I need to define the word anointing. As we have already seen from the discussion of anointing with oil, the word *anoint* means to *rub* or to *smear*. But the anointing of the Holy Ghost involves more than just being dabbed with olive oil.

Anointing in this sense means the power of God in demonstration. It is the presence and activity of God to achieve a particular purpose. Many times, this anointing is present for the purpose of healing the sick. Acts 10:38 says:

...how God anointed Jesus of Nazareth with the Holy Spirit and with power, who went about doing good and healing all who were oppressed by the devil, for God was with Him.

As we have already seen from 1 John 2:20, every believer has an anointing that abides within them. But apparently there are some who are anointed in a particular way to minister to the sick that goes beyond the ordinary.

We see this in Jesus' ministry in Luke 6:17-19:

And He came down with them and stood on a level place with a crowd of His disciples and a great multitude of people from all Judea and Jerusalem, and from the seacoast of Tyre and Sidon, who came to hear Him and be healed of their diseases, as well as those who were tormented with unclean spirits. And they were healed. And the whole multitude sought to touch Him, for power went out from Him and healed them all.

Jesus also told His disciples in John 14:12 that they would do greater works than He did. The healing virtue coming out of Peter was so strong that there were occasions when his shadow passing over people caused them to be healed, as in Acts 5:15-16:

...so that they brought the sick out into the streets and laid them on beds and couches, that at least the shadow of Peter passing by might fall on some of them. Also a multitude gathered from the surrounding cities to Jerusalem, bringing sick people and those who were tormented by unclean spirits, and they were all healed.

In Acts 19:11-12 we see other special miracles occurring:

Now God worked unusual miracles by the hands of Paul, so that even handkerchiefs or aprons were brought from his body to the sick, and the diseases left them and the evil spirits went out of them.

We still use what are known as prayer cloths to minister to the sick. Some of the most unusual miracles of healing happen as a result. There is nothing about the cloth itself that is magical or that has curative powers, but when a cloth has been saturated with the presence of the healing anointing, it can have the same effect as the laying on of hands.

Some of the most remarkable healings ever recorded have happened as a result of those who have been specially anointed to minister to the sick. John G. Lake, missionary to Africa, saw plague germs die when placed upon his hand under a microscope. The healing anointing of God killed the bacteria immediately.

Stephen Jeffreys, a Welsh minister who was instrumental in the early days of Pentecost in Britain, had an unusual anointing to minister to those who were afflicted with rheumatoid arthritis. Eyewitnesses said they saw limbs that were literally twisted like pretzels straighten out instantly under his ministry.

We thank God for all those who are specially anointed to minister to the sick, but we don't have to wait until one of them comes to town to be healed. We must never exalt a person or a gift above the Word of God. There is one way to be healed that God has provided that is available to everyone at any time, regardless of who you are, where you live or how desperate your condition.

During Jesus' ministry, healing occurred over and over again when individuals exercised faith for healing themselves. We understand that supernatural manifestations of God's healing power was evident in Jesus' ministry, yet in many cases, Jesus Himself acknowledged that it was an individual's faith that made them well. In other cases, it was someone who was either related to or closely associated with the one needing healing who exercised their faith on behalf of the sick person.

Here are some examples of people believing God for themselves and seeing the results of their faith:

Matthew 9:27-30: *When Jesus departed from there, two blind men followed Him, crying out and saying, "Son of David, have mercy on us!" And when He had come into the house, the blind men came to Him. And Jesus said to them, "Do you believe that I am able to do this?" They said to Him, "Yes, Lord." Then He touched their eyes,* *saying, "According to your faith let it be to you." And their eyes were opened...*

Matthew 20:29-34: *Now as they went out of Jericho, a great multitude followed Him. And behold, two blind men sitting by the road, when they heard that Jesus was passing by, cried out, saying, "Have mercy on us, O Lord, Son of David!" Then the multitude warned them that they should be quiet; but they cried out all the more, saying, "Have mercy on us, O Lord, Son of David!" So Jesus stood still and called them, and said, "What do you want Me to do for you?" They said to Him, "Lord, that our eyes may be opened." So Jesus had compassion and touched their eyes. And immediately their eyes received sight, and they followed Him.*

Mark 5:25-34: *Now a certain woman had a flow of blood for twelve years, and had suffered many things from many physicians. She had spent all that she had and was no better, but rather grew worse. When she heard about Jesus, she came behind Him in the crowd and touched His garment. For she said, "If only I may touch His clothes, I shall be made well." Immediately the fountain of* *her blood was dried up, and she felt in her body that she was healed of the affliction. And Jesus, immediately knowing in Himself that power had gone out of Him, turned around in the crowd and said, "Who touched My clothes?" But His disciples said to Him, "You see the multitude thronging You, and You say, 'Who touched Me?' "And He looked around to see her who had done this thing. But the woman, fearing and trembling, knowing what had happened to her, came and fell down before Him and told Him the whole truth. And He said to her, "Daughter, your faith has made you well. Go in peace, and be healed of your affliction.*

Luke 17:11-19: *Now it happened as He went to Jerusalem that He passed through the midst of Samaria and Galilee. Then as He entered a certain village, there met Him ten men who were lepers, who stood afar off. And they lifted up their voices and said, "Jesus, Master, have mercy on us!" So when He saw them, He said to them, "Go, show yourselves to the priests." And so it was that as they went, they were cleansed. And one of them, when he saw that he was healed, returned, and with a loud voice glorified God, and fell down on* *his face at His feet, giving Him thanks. And he was a Samaritan. So Jesus answered and said, "Were there not ten cleansed? But where are the nine? Were there not any found who returned to give glory to God except this foreigner?" And He said to him, "Arise, go your way. Your faith has made you well.*

In other cases, the person needing healing may not have had faith, but someone close to them did, as in these examples:

Matthew 8:5-13: *Now when Jesus had entered Capernaum, a centurion came to Him, pleading with Him, saying, "Lord, my servant is lying at home paralyzed, dreadfully tormented." And Jesus said to him, "I will come and heal him." The centurion answered and said, "Lord, I am not worthy that You should come under my roof. But only speak a word, and my servant will be healed. For I also am a man under authority, having soldiers under me. And I say to this one, 'Go,' and he goes; and to another, 'Come,' and he comes; and to my servant, 'Do this,' and he does it." When Jesus heard it, He marveled, and said to those who followed, "Assuredly, I say to you, I have not found such great faith, not even in Israel! And I say to* *you that many will come from east and west, and sit down with Abraham, Isaac, and Jacob in the kingdom of heaven. But the sons of the kingdom will be cast out into outer darkness. There will be weeping and gnashing of teeth." Then Jesus said to the centurion, "Go your way; and as you have believed, so let it be done for you." And his servant was healed that same hour.*

Luke 5:17-26: *Now it happened on a certain day, as He was teaching, that there were Pharisees and teachers of the law sitting by, who had come out of every town of Galilee, Judea, and Jerusalem. And the power of the Lord was present to heal them. Then behold, men brought on a bed a man who was paralyzed, whom they sought to bring in and lay before Him. And when they could not find how they might bring him in, because of the crowd, they went up on the housetop and let him down with his bed through the tiling into the midst before Jesus. When He saw their faith, He said to him, "Man, your sins are forgiven you." And the scribes and the Pharisees began to reason, saying, "Who is this who speaks blasphemies? Who can forgive sins but God alone?" But when Jesus perceived their thoughts, He answered and said to* *them, "Why are you reasoning in your hearts? Which is easier, to say, 'Your sins are forgiven you,' or to say, 'Rise up and walk'? But that you may know that the Son of Man has power on earth to forgive sins" — He said to the man who was paralyzed, "I say to you, arise, take up your bed, and go to your house." Immediately he rose up before them, took up what he had been lying on, and departed to his own house, glorifying God. And they were all amazed, and they glorified God and were filled with fear, saying, "We have seen strange things today!"*

John 4:46-53: *So Jesus came again to Cana of Galilee where He had made the water wine. And there was a certain nobleman whose son was sick at Capernaum. When he heard that Jesus had come out of Judea into Galilee, he went to Him and implored Him to come down and heal his son, for he was at the point of death. Then Jesus said to him, "Unless you people see signs and wonders, you will by no means believe." The nobleman said to Him, "Sir, come down before my child dies!" Jesus said to him, "Go your way; your son lives." So the man believed the word that Jesus spoke to him, and he went his way. And as he was now going*

*down, his servants met him and told him, saying,
"Your son lives!" Then he inquired of them the
hour when he got better. And they said to him,
"Yesterday at the seventh hour the fever left him."
So the father knew that it was at the same hour in
which Jesus said to him, "Your son lives." And he
himself believed, and his whole household.*

Believing God yourself for healing will work
for anyone at any time. Why, then, don't more
people do it?

Some don't do it because they don't know
about it — they've never heard that God wants
them to be well. Some don't do it because they
have an entitlement mentality, as I mentioned earlier. Some people don't believe God for healing
because they think it would take too much time
and effort.

But as someone said, you're either going to
spend time believing God to be well or you'll
spend time in the doctor's office trying to get well.
Which would you rather do?

For some, faith is equated to religious relics
and superstitious beliefs of a bygone era. But faith
is a necessary part of the daily life of every Christian. Hebrews 11:6 says:

But without faith it is impossible to please Him, for he who comes to God must believe that He is, and that He is a rewarder of those who diligently seek Him.

Second Corinthians 5:7 says:

For we walk by faith, not by sight.

Galatians 3:11 says:

But that no one is justified by the law in the sight of God is evident, for "the just shall live by faith."

If faith is such an essential principle for a successful Christian life, we should know more about it. A thorough treatment of the subject is the study of a lifetime, but let me just give you a few fundamentals about faith.

The best definition of faith I have ever heard came from my pastor, Dr. Lester Sumrall. I was sharing a meal with him after he had visited our church for the first time, and I apologized that our building was totally inadequate to hold the people who came to hear him. We didn't even have a place to put his book table.

I told him I needed more faith so we could build a bigger building. He looked across the table with those ice-blue eyes of his and said, "You don't need more faith. You need to know what faith is."

I thought about responding with all the things I had heard about faith in Bible classes and from my own study, but then I remembered that I was talking to someone who was casting out demons in the mountains of Tibet long before I was born. I prudently held my peace and waited to see how he would define faith. After all, he was obviously someone who knew what it was from experience!

"Faith," he said to me, "is knowing God."

The longer I live, the more sense that definition makes. Faith is confidence and trust. In order to have faith in someone, you have to know what they said.

To know what God said, we have to know His Word, the Bible. And to know the Bible, we have to read it, not casually, but diligently. Romans 10:17 says:

So then faith comes by hearing, and hearing by the word of God.

In addition to knowing the Word of God, we must also know the God of the Word. Sometimes people memorize the letter of the law, but fail to understand the spirit of the law, and cause more harm than good. In the words of Jesus, they strain out a gnat and swallow a camel, and risk alienating people with their dogmatic doctrines rather than allowing love and grace to be the motivation for their words and actions.

The only way to get to know anyone better is to spend time with them. You can ask all of a person's friends and acquaintances for their opinions of them, but at best your knowledge of them will be second-hand.

If you really want to know someone, you have to talk to them yourself, and give them the opportunity to respond to you. Generally speaking, the more time you spend with someone, the better you will get to know them.

In order to have faith, we need to know God, and in order to know God, we have to spend time with Him. The very thought makes some people uncomfortable. But the better we know God, the more likely it is that we will believe what He says, and we will see our faith in Him grow and develop. Jesus said in Mark 10:27:

> …*With men it is impossible, but not with God; for with God all things are possible.*

HEALED: ONCE AND FOR ALL

Divine healing may seem like an impossibility to you or to someone you know, but I can assure you — with God all things are possible. I encourage you to find out more about the God of the Bible and let your faith in Him develop. What seems impossible will move out of the realm of hopes and dreams and into reality.

God revealed Himself to the children of Israel as a healer at their departure from Egypt. He brought them out by giving them strength in their physical bodies so they could make the trek from Goshen to the land of promise. But immediately after they saw the pursuing Egyptian army overthrown by the waters of the Red Sea, they encountered a difficulty they hadn't faced before — the water in the wilderness was bitter and undrinkable.

I remember the chaos that occurred in old western movies when the cattle smelled water and began to stampede. There was no holding them back as they thundered toward the water hole. I can only imagine what it must have been like to try to hold six million people back from trying to get a drink at an oasis full of alkali water.

Moses cried out to the Lord, and God told him to cast a tree into the water. The bitter water was immediately made sweet, and God said in Exodus 15:26:

If you diligently heed the voice of the Lord your God and do what is right in His sight, give ear to

His commandments and keep all His statutes, I will put none of the diseases on you which I have brought on the Egyptians. For I am the Lord who heals you.

The word *heals* here is the same word translated *physician* elsewhere in the Old Testament. God was telling His people He would be their physician, and that when they needed healing, they could depend upon Him for help and cure.

Psalm 103:1-5 echoes this same sentiment, along with other benefits God provides for His people:

Bless the Lord, O my soul; and all that is within me, bless His holy name! Bless the Lord, O my soul, and forget not all His benefits: Who forgives all your iniquities, Who heals all your diseases, Who redeems your life from destruction, Who crowns you with lovingkindness and tender mercies, Who satisfies your mouth with good things, So that your youth is renewed like the eagle's.

The Israelites had seen the results of rebellion to God's will as plague after plague was poured out upon the Egyptians. God wanted them to know that it was not His intention to do them anything but good as they made their way to a land He had provided for them.

God even gave them special dietary laws to help them remain healthy. Most of the things He restricted them from eating were things you wouldn't want to eat anyway — buzzards and bats, eels and cats and the like.

There were times when it was hard for them to recognize God as the Healer — especially when they encountered difficulties and even death as a result of their own rebellion.

We have been redeemed from the curse of sickness. We have no doubt of that from the record of God's Word both in the Old and New Testaments. But just as the children of Israel at times complained that God was trying to kill them in the wilderness, sometimes people today are tempted to think that God is the one making them sick and even killing them.

They have a hard time recognizing God as a healer because of their experience. Then, in the middle of their pain and suffering, the devil comes along and reminds them of stories they have heard in the Bible about two men who suffered as well.

I want to talk about those men and what they went through.

Any discussion of divine healing will inevitably include questions about what seem to be exceptions to healing in the Bible. Some who oppose the doctrine of healing are quick to point these things out as proof that God doesn't heal any longer. Others approach these things with a more open mind, and genuinely want to know what happened so they can understand the truth.

The first case involves Job. For generations Job has been held up by some as an example of how God is glorified in sickness, because, after all, Job was a righteous man who maintained his integrity even though he lost everything and had boils all over his body.

A careful reading of the first two chapters of Job reveal that it was not God that robbed Job of his possessions, killed his children and struck him with a loathsome physical condition. In fact, Satan complained that he couldn't get to Job because God had placed a hedge of protection around him. But something happened to cause a breach in that hedge, because Job 2:7 says:

So Satan went out from the presence of the Lord, and struck Job with painful boils from the sole of his foot to the crown of his head.

It's bad enough that Job had to suffer as he did. What made his suffering even worse was his three "friends" came to comfort him, and instead accused Job of doing all kinds of things that he didn't do. They reasoned that the only way Job could be going through such a tragedy was if he had done some heinous thing or harbored ill in his heart toward God or others.

It's no secret that sin has consequences, yet that truth has been disregarded or forgotten altogether in our fast-paced, feel-good world. You wouldn't know it from the messages that are so prevalent in popular culture, but it's really no surprise that people who are sexually promiscuous have a higher incidence of sexually transmitted diseases. Their lifestyle choices are in many cases a direct link to health problems that others don't have.

It's no wonder that people who have been lifelong smokers have a higher incidence of lung cancer, or those who consume alcohol intemperately have liver problems. If you consume more calories than you burn, you'll gain weight. If you like deep fried pastries three times a day, it might be an indication that you are a candidate for vascular problems or heart disease. So it should come as no surprise that there are times when sin is directly responsible for illness.

But just because someone is sick doesn't mean they have sinned, and it was unfair of Job's friends to make that assumption. It was apparently a widely held belief even in New Testament times.

The disciples asked Jesus about a blind man in John 9:2-3, 6-7:

> *"Rabbi, who sinned, this man or his parents, that he was born blind?" Jesus answered, "Neither this man nor his parents sinned, but that the works of God should be revealed in him... When He had said these things, He spat on the ground and made clay with the saliva; and He anointed the eyes of the blind man with the clay. And He said to him, "Go, wash in the pool of Siloam" (which is translated, Sent). So he went and washed, and came back seeing."*

Jesus didn't want to debate who sinned or even whether someone sinned — His purpose was to restore the man's sight, which He did without delay.

Sin obviously wasn't Job's problem — listen to what God Himself had to say in Job 1:8:

> *Then the Lord said to Satan, "Have you considered My servant Job, that there is none like him on the earth, a blameless and upright man, one who fears God and shuns evil?"*

We don't know what caused the hedge of protection around Job to come down, but what we can say with assurance is that it was Satan who struck him, not God. The last chapter of Job reveals that God is the one who blessed Job at the end of this episode, and gave him twice as much as he had before. The message is clear — Satan is the accuser and the one who brings a curse; God is the redeemer and the one who brings blessing.

The next example that is used by some to try to prove that God doesn't always heal is Paul. In 2 Corinthians 12:7, Paul relates how he was given a thorn in the flesh:

> *And lest I should be exalted above measure by the abundance of the revelations, a thorn in the flesh*

*was given to me, a messenger of Satan to buffet me,
lest I be exalted above measure.*

Some Bible scholars have taken this to mean
that Paul had a disease, and others have even gone
to great lengths to describe its effects on Paul's
body.

Paul does talk about his infirmities, but that
word means *weaknesses*, and isn't always used to
describe sickness. I suppose we could excuse Paul
for having some infirmities — after all, he was
stoned and left for dead, shipwrecked, snake bitten
and subjected to exposure and hardship of every
sort as he traveled throughout the Roman Empire
to preach the Gospel.

There is no evidence that this thorn in the
flesh of which Paul spoke had anything to do with
a sickness or disease. In fact, there is abundant
evidence to the contrary. The word *flesh* as it is
used in 2 Corinthians 12:7 doesn't always mean
muscle tissue; it can also mean *human nature*, with
all that implies. Paul wasn't talking about a literal
wound in his body.

Paul goes on to describe just what it was that
was causing him this problem. He said it was a

messenger of Satan. The word *messenger* here is the Greek word *angelos*, often translated *angel*.

Paul said it was a messenger of Satan or a demon spirit. It was sent to buffet him, which means to strike him with blow after blow. The purpose of this buffeting was to prevent him from being exalted above measure, or thinking too highly of himself as a result of the visions and revelations he had received.

When the term *thorn in the flesh* is used elsewhere in the Bible, it always refers to *people*, never to sickness or disease. (See Numbers 33:55, Joshua 23:13, and Judges 2:1-3.)

So the next time someone tells you that they have a thorn in the flesh, ask them if they can identify the person who is causing them such trouble. Or you can ask them to tell you what abundance of revelation they have received that would cause them to have such a thorn assigned to them.

In both cases, they probably won't know how to answer you. You can tell them you'll be happy to pull out their thorn by sharing the truth with them.

Here's another excuse people repeat about why they are sick: "God's just trying to teach me something." And here's the question I always ask in response: "What have you learned?"

Most of the time people who have this attitude say they are learning patience. Of course, you can learn to be patient without being sick, and I've encountered many sick folks who were anything but patient. To accuse God, the ultimate loving Father, of putting sickness on His people to teach them something is the equivalent of accusing Him of child abuse.

Sometimes people will say they are hospitalized to be a witness to those they encounter there. I always remind them that there is a door for visitors at the hospital, not just for patients. Besides, their witness will be a whole lot more effective if they are well and not sick.

The objections to healing go on and on — Timothy took a little wine for his stomach's sake; Trophimus was left at Miletum sick and so forth. It surprises me how diligently people will look for a reason to be ill instead of well.

This tendency probably underscores the biggest objection to the doctrine of divine healing, and that is people's experience. Disease is a fact of the human condition, and has been ever since sin entered the world in Genesis chapter 3.

It's hard for many of us living in our modern culture to remember the apprehension previous generations had due to the prevalence of diseases that are virtually unknown today. Even something as commonplace as the flu was a killer responsible for millions of deaths in previous generations.

We can all thank God for the inspired work of those in the field of medicine who have labored and sacrificed to develop treatments and procedures that can make our lives longer and healthier. But every time a new drug is developed, it seems as though we hear about another disease or strain of disease that was previously unknown that creates yet another health challenge.

I have never said we should not take advantage of the benefits medical science has to offer. I certainly do not subscribe to the misinformed view that medicine is contrary to God. Most medical professionals I have met are awed by the complexity and intricacy of the human body, and many of them recognize that they are limited in what they know and what they can do.

What I am saying is that regardless of the advantages modern medicine has to offer, we still need to trust God to keep our bodies well and working at their optimum capacity.

Let me say this very clearly — if you are under a doctor's care for any kind of physical condition, don't stop what you're doing and say you're believing God. Don't stop taking your medication, or wearing your eyeglasses or anything else that may have been prescribed for you.

Well-meaning but ill-advised people have died because they stopped taking their prescriptions or threw away their health aids and said they were believing God. That is foolishness, not faith.

As your faith grows, God will do a work in your body that is great enough that your doctor will notice it. God is not hindered by medication, and refusing to take pills or other treatment is not an act of faith.

Most, if not all of us will experience some form of physical infirmity at some point in our lives. How can we reconcile our experience with what we see in the Bible and believe to be the will of God regarding our physical well-being?

THE GREAT PHYSICIAN

I tell people not to adjust their theology in the midst of a crisis. The Word of God is true regardless of our experience or the experience of others. If you set out on a journey and stop or turn around every time you encounter a delay or a detour, you will have a hard time ever reaching your destination. In the same way, if you become discouraged about trusting God every time you experience a contrary symptom, it's unlikely you will ever experience His healing power.

If you or someone you know is sick, talking about healing is not a criticism of your faith or theirs. Many genuine saints of God have died because of the onset of some sickness or disease, and they were saved and on their way to heaven.

The time or manner of their death in no way nullifies their salvation. But how much better would it have been if they had the advantage of knowing what the Bible says about healing?

Some folks have a lot of religious tradition and years of doubt and unbelief to overcome when it comes to the subject of divine healing. It may not always be possible for them to develop their faith to deal with a serious health problem in time, but I believe it's still worth making the effort.

It can be very helpful to have friends or family members who will stand with you in faith, but even if you don't have that kind of support, God will honor your own faith and your steadfastness. I will always encourage you to believe God for His best, and to receive every benefit He has provided for you.

Let me explain it this way. When you were a child, you probably looked forward to Christmas Day. If you had the experience that most families did, you had some sort of gift exchange to celebrate the occasion.

You always looked for the packages that had your name on them, and you anticipated opening them to see what you received. You made sure to open each one, and may have even looked around to see if there was anything you had missed.

You were happy about each and every gift, even though it may not have been exactly what you wanted or thought you needed. You never left a package with your name on it unopened.

If your parents pointed out a gift that you missed, you never said you didn't want it, or that you had opened enough gifts for one day. If you had, your family would have thought there was something wrong with you.

In the same way, God has provided gifts for you as your Creator and Redeemer. One of those gifts is forgiveness of sin. Another is healing. There are many more, of course.

As children of God, we should never refuse anything He sacrificed to provide for us, or say we don't want it or need it. To do so would be ungrateful, to say the least. But many of God's kids say that salvation from sin is all they need, and they don't want to know about any of the other gifts God has graciously provided.

God paid a great price to provide healing for us. We should never ignore the gift of healing God has so generously given. He has redeemed us from sickness once for all.

ABOUT THE AUTHOR

ROD PARSLEY, bestselling author of more than sixty books, is the dynamic pastor of World Harvest Church in Columbus, Ohio, a church with worldwide ministries and a global outreach. As a highly sought-after crusade and conference speaker whom God has raised up as a prophetic voice to America and the world, Parsley is calling people to Jesus Christ through the good news of the Gospel.

He oversees Bridge of Hope Missions, Harvest Preparatory School, World Harvest Bible College, and the *Breakthrough* broadcast, a television and radio show seen by millions and broadcast to nearly 200 countries around the world, including a potential viewing audience of 97% of the homes in the United States and 78% in Canada. *Breakthrough* is carried on 1,400 stations and cable affiliates, including the Trinity Broadcasting Network, the Canadian Vision Network, Armed Forces Radio and Television Network, and in several countries spanning the globe.

Parsley's refreshingly direct style encourages Christians to examine and eradicate sin from their lives. A fearless champion of living God's way, Parsley follows the high standard set by Jesus Christ and compels his readers to do the same. He and his wife Joni have two children, Ashton and Austin.

For more information about *Breakthrough*,
World Harvest Church, World Harvest Bible College,
Harvest Preparatory School, The Center for Moral
Clarity, or to receive a product list of the many books,
CDs, and DVDs by Rod Parsley, write or call:

BREAKTHROUGH/WORLD HARVEST CHURCH
P.O. Box 100
Columbus, OH 43216-0100 USA
(866) 241-4292
www.RodParsley.com

WORLD HARVEST BIBLE COLLEGE
P.O. Box 32901
Columbus, OH 43232-0901 USA
(614) 837-4088
www.RodParsley.com

HARVEST PREPARATORY SCHOOL
P.O. Box 32903
Columbus, OH 43232-0903 USA
(614) 837-1990
www.RodParsley.com

THE CENTER FOR MORAL CLARITY
P.O. Box 100
Columbus, OH 43216-0100 USA
(614) 382-1188
cmc.RodParsley.com

If you need prayer, Breakthrough Prayer Warriors are
ready to pray with you 24 hours a day, 7 days a week at
(866) 241-4292